P9-CCQ-653

YELLOWSTONE
SELECTED PHOTOGRAPHS
1870 - 1960

Yellowstone

SELECTED PHOTOGRAPHS
1870-1960

Foreword by Senator Alan Simpson

Edited by Carl Schreier

HOMESTEAD PUBLISHING
Moose, Wyoming

Copyright © 1989 by Carl Schreier
All rights reserved
Photographic credits may be found on page 107

ISBN 0-943972-11-6 (paperback)
ISBN 0-943972-12-4 (hardback)
Library of Congress Catalog Card Number 88-80159
Manufactured in the United States of America

Published by
H O M E S T E A D   P U B L I S H I N G
Box 193
Moose, Wyoming 83012

Front cover photograph:
*An automobile in the trial trip around the
Park prior to admission of private autos, 1915*
photo by J.E. Haynes, courtesy National Park Service,
Yellowstone National Park

Back cover photograph:
Tower Falls and towers, 1917
photo by J.E. Haynes, Haynes Foundation Collection,
Montana Historical Society

Preface photograph:
*View from Capitol Hill toward Mt. Everts, showing
Fort Yellowstone installation of U.S. Army, 1895*
photo by F.J. Haynes, courtesy National Archives

FOR GOLDIE, WITH LOVE

FOREWORD

The Simpson and Burnett families have been living there in the sun and shadow of Yellowstone Park since the late 1880s. And before that, my dad's grandfather — Finn Burnett — arrived in South Pass City in the 1870s. The family has always felt a great gravitational pull to the Park. It seems we always lived next to Yellowstone. The family heritage can be found deeply rooted in both of Wyoming's gateways to Yellowstone – Cody and Jackson.

Yellowstone Park — the wildlife, the lakes, the extraordinary geological features, the magic of it all — is woven into the very fabric of Simpson family history.

My dear dad, Milward L. Simpson, was born in Jackson Hole on November 12, 1897. Not many born there that year! Several streets in Jackson are named after Dad's family. Simpson Street itself. Virginia Street named after Dad's sister, Glenwood was Dad's brother, Pearl a great aunt. Dad has his own street there, too — and it's a great thrill to this day to stand at the corner of Millward and Simpson. Dad always said the Highway Department gave him a good tussle or two when he was governor — and then even after he was out of office, he said, "By gad, they also misspelled my name on the street sign!"

My grandparents, William L. Simpson and Margaret L. Simpson "Popoo" and "Nanny" to all the grandkids — shared with us so many stories of how it was in the early days of Jackson and Yellowstone. They spent some awfully cold, severe winters in a little log building heated by just one wood-burning stove and a fireplace. Trips into Pinedale and Rock Springs were exceptionally long, tough hauls in the wintertime. The family stayed pretty close to the hearth during those winter months.

For their winter food supply they relied almost totally upon wild game. In more recent times when we prepared a dinner of venison or elk, my dear grandmother would say, "Wait a minute, not for me. I spent the first 50 years of my life living on elk, deer, fish, duck, rabbit, sage hen and pheasant. I'll take a nice piece of beef, thank you." And so it was.

Popoo was a lawyer of the old school. He had been thrown out of the fourth grade for witnessing a public hanging, but he continued his studies, and the law had taken its hold on him. He met my grandmother while she was still a very young lady — teaching the Indians at the St. Stephens school near Riverton. He knew one had to have some basic Latin in order to practice law in those times, so Nanny taught him some Latin phrases and that started him off in the legal profession. He proved to be one of the most unique and remarkable lawyers in Wyoming. His magnificent native guile, cunning and craft made him damned near unbeatable.

Popoo died in December of 1940 — of a broken heart. His son, my father, Milward, had run for the United States Senate in November 1940. He was beaten soundly by the incumbent, Senator Joseph O'Mahoney. Popoo had started a citizens group called "Democrats for Simpson". Dad suffered through that defeat and handled it beautifully, but Popoo died within a month after the election. He was buried that winter — his grave literally blasted from the frozen earth of Snow King Mountain, which was then known as Simpson's Ridge.

Having gone through that sad process in the middle of winter, Nanny declared that if she died in winter, "Just have me cremated and then take me up there next to Billy on some beautiful summer day." As it happened she lived to be 100, passing away in March 1974. But true to her wishes, we buried her ashes at that mountain site on a magnificent June day in Jackson. From my dear grandparents final resting place, one can see the tips of the Tetons sticking up over East Gros Ventre Butte.

While brother Pete and I were children, we frequently traveled through Yellowstone on trips from our home in Cody to visit with my grandparents in Jackson. The Park was an absolute fantasy land for us. When Popoo died, my dad determined that he should go to Jackson the following summer to wind up his father's law practice. When school ended in Cody in May 1941, we headed for Jackson and lived in the Woodbury House, about a mile from Moose. That remarkable and extraordinary lady, Mardy Murie, lives there now. She is a woman who brings such an awesome degree of commitment, zest and spirit to her community and our environment. The place rings with memories.

Brother Pete and I had a young lad's curiosity and spirit when we lived in that lovely home. We fished in the Snake River and on Flat Creek under the rim of the Tetons. When school started up in early September, we went to the Moose School, which was on the road between Moose and the White Grass Ranch. It was about a mile away from our house. The foundation of that little schoolhouse is still there and I have shown my own children that very spot in later years.

Soon after Halloween of `41 — and before the snows came we left and returned to Cody. The Park was exquisite in November. As we drove home through the Park, we felt as if we had it all to ourselves — but for the magnificent birds and animals.

Yellowstone is so beautiful, breathtaking and unique in all its moods. Ann and I have spent a New Year's Eve in Yellowstone Park and watched Old Faithful huff and puff itself in a hoary white arc into what appeared to be the very stratosphere — what I thought was a vapor and ice cloud literally hundreds of feet in the sky. The experience was enhanced by the excitement that it was 37 degrees below zero and, yes, with a full moon — one that the fairy tale cow could never have jumped over! Ah, yes. That one is etched back there in the retina of my eye and mind — in spades.

And now my dear children make their periodic pilgrimages to the Park. Mom and dad used to take us there after work on Friday evenings. We would sit bundled up on the shore of Yellowstone Lake and fry up some steaks and potatoes and sing – Mom, Dad, Pete and I. How does one forget those things? Thank heaven we never do or ever want to. My dear dad and mother still love to be bundled up snuggly and taken there.

As a boy, I also clearly remember sitting on the front porch of our home in Cody, which faced west to the Yellowstone Highway. I would watch those sleek and dazzling bright yellow White Motor Company buses go into the Park. At that age I had never seen a vehicle more beautiful than those buses with the big Yellowstone Park Company seal on the side — those huge tires and the passengers sitting up there so high off the road in absolute luxury. Shades of Mr. Toad! The visions of a little boy.

We now travel the Park in more modern transport, but that awesome magnetism of Yellowstone Park will never change. It has a special energy that strongly and purposefully draws one back — winter, summer, fall or spring. And now, here we see it brought to life once again in this fine book. We know that it was originally established in 1872 as "a pleasuring ground for the enjoyment of the people". That is the language of the Organic Act creating it. How fitting.

Whether I am in Washington — or wherever — I always have Yellowstone Park in a corner of my heart and in the treasure hoard of my mind. So it is with all the generations of Simpsons and

Burnetts. It is a rich heritage of gritty and courageous people who came to this rugged state in the 1870s and 1880s. They chose to make this country their home. Their space. This slice of the earth has a powerful draw on us all as it continually enriches our lives.

This fine author now enriches our lives anew by presenting these vivid photos. It only impresses upon us again what a magic land it was, is, and ever shall be. God's noblest natural creation.

Senator Alan Simpson
Washington, D.C.

INTRODUCTION

In a brown, leather grain family album is an old black and white photograph of my father and brother in Yellowstone National Park. My father is dressed in khaki cotton pants and a flight jacket, leaning back against a log rail. Beside him stands my brother, eight years old, with his Wrangler jean cuffs rolled-up, sporting an Indian headdress. Between them, and beyond the rail fence, plunges the cataract of the Lower Falls of the Yellowstone River.

The year was 1956 — the year I entered the world. It was the period when dark-colored humpback automobiles were progressing into gleaming multicolored, finned 'classics'. But most importantly it was the closing of a romantic age. The picture captured, what is to me, the end of a by-gone era. An era of nearly 100 years of romanticism, glamour, and bliss. This era, or "golden age", captured during the reign of black and white photography, ended with the advent of color Kodachromes.

Black and white photography and Yellowstone have gone hand in hand through this golden age. Since photography's earliest origin in France, during the mid nineteenth century, there have been efforts by photographers to express a romantic fascination with the exotic and a mania for fact gathering and documentation. Exotic lands — the monuments of Egypt, the harshness of the Antarctic, the geysers of Yellowstone — became subjects of sponsors for early expeditions in order to obtain documentation of their existence. However the photographers were artists who produced work that to modern eyes appears touched with poetic simplicity.

The photographs which comprise this collection were collected from major archives and museums which house Western historical photographs. They were edited with the intent of illustrating Yellowstone's history and the country's changing social environment. They also show Yellowstone's unique landforms — geysers, canyons, meadows, valleys, mountains, lakes and waterfalls — to the procession of those who came to view these wonders — explorers, soldiers, presidents, tourists, coach drivers, thermal spring bathers and rangers.

Through this golden age three prominent photographers stood out among the procession. William Henry Jackson (1843-1942), Frank Jay Haynes (1853-1921), and his son Jack Ellis Haynes (1884-1962) documented an evolving Yellowstone.

And Yellowstone did evolve. Decade by decade Yellowstone has been influenced by worldly events. Changing fashions, architecture, foods, transportation, habits and attitudes all contribute to this evolution caught by the eye of the camera.

Yellowstone was created in 1872 by an act of Congress. The region was an isolated unheard of tract of land in Wyoming Territory. One Congressman even stated during the floor debate that "This bill treads upon no rights of the settler, infringes upon no permanent prospect of settlement of that Territory." The area seemed so remote and far removed from everyday life that the bill passed with little opposition creating Yellowstone and our first national park.

That first decade of the 1870s not only saw the establishment of Yellowstone National Park but also the founding of John D. Rockefeller's Standard Oil Company; the premiere of P.T. Barnum's Circus, "The Greatest Show on Earth"; the reelection of Ulysses S. Grant in spite of public scandals during his administration (Grant's signature of the Yellowstone Park Act created Yellowstone); and the establishment of the first American zoo in Philadelphia.

This initial decade was also important in that Yellowstone was "rediscovered" by private and then government-led expeditions leading to its proposal for protection. A government sponsored expedition brought the first photographer, William Henry Jackson, to Yellowstone which led to the subsequent first photographs at Mammoth Hot Springs in 1871 (page 2).

William Jackson was raised in New York state, soldiered in the Civil War, and worked as a bullwhacker herding oxen and mustangs across the plains of Wyoming and Utah. He began his professional career in 1868 when he established his photographic studio in Omaha, Nebraska. Omaha was the home of the Union Pacific Railroad, and the period was alive with the railroad-building race to connect east and west with a transcontinental railroad. The railroad provided Jackson access to the frontier and its unique Western views. And views of Cheyenne, of the Great Salt Lake Valley, and of Weber and Echo canyons became available at his Omaha studio.

These Western views interested Dr. Ferdinand Hayden, director of the U. S. Geological Survey of the Territories, prompting him to call upon Jackson at his studio in July 1870. Hayden appointed Jackson offical photographer, and he became one of the regular branches of the Survey's operations, photographing Yellowstone's landscapes during three offical survey expeditons, 1871, 1872 and 1878.

For a photographer, photographic processes during this period were time-consuming and cumbersome. Jackson brought three cameras along on the first expedition — a six-and-a-half by eight-and-a-half, an eight by ten and a stereoscopic camera. For photographic development he was required to carry a portable dark chamber for performing chemical procedures on a glass plate immediately before and after each exposure. Thus, the largest number of negatives Jackson produced in a single day was seventeen, a record for wet plate work.

Jackson's photographs, along with artist Thomas Moran's sketches and paintings, and the reports and documents submitted by Hayden played an important role in the protection and establishment of Yellowstone as a national park.

After the survey years of the 1870s, the next decade saw internal strife and growth for Yellowstone. Still remote, unheard of, it was a great distance to travel for Easterners or urban socialites. But during this time the streets in New York were first being lit by electricity; Robert Louis Stevenson's book, *Treasure Island*, emerged; the Statue of Liberty was dedicated; and North and South Dakota, Montana and Washington became states. Here in Yellowstone the few visitors who entered the park chipped away at the thermal mineral deposits while poachers took their toll on wildlife for their hides, heads and meat.

Other problems occurred when superintendents and administrators conspired with private concessions when granting leases. Buildings were erected near, sometimes on, the features the Park was established to protect. These increasing problems prompted the Secretary of Interior in 1886 to call upon the Secretary of War for assistance in administrating the Park. For three decades, the Army remained vigilant and protective of the Park's resources. They established Fort Yellowstone (page ii) and a network of soldier stations (page 25) in remote regions of the Park only a day's ski, bicycle or horseback ride apart. A path, then a trail and eventually a road, in the configuration of two loops connected these stations. The 1880s also saw the introduction of photographer F. Jay Haynes.

After growing up in Michigan, F. Jay Haynes began his career at the age of 21 as an illustration salesman in Beaver Dam, Wisconsin. Later, he became an apprentice photographer at Lockwood's

Temple of Photography in Ripon, Wisconsin. This apprenticeship gave him the knowledge and expertise in plate preparation and print making along with the fundamentals of business. His horse-drawn "view wagon", which took him to rural areas for portraits, farm and landscape views, provided the basis for his future endeavors.

Haynes struck out on his own and with a loan he established his studio in Moorehead, Minnesota. From there he began touring the "bonanza farms" of the Red River Valley. Run under the auspices of the Northern Pacific Railroad, these productive farms of five to thirty thousand acres could yield an average of twenty-two bushels of wheat to the acre. Soon, the Northern Pacific began hiring Haynes for promotional photographs. This first connection with the railroad was to become a lucrative business association lasting for nearly forty years.

The railroad began sending Haynes on excursions to the Black Hills, the Missouri River, the Badlands, and into Canada. And by 1881 Haynes ventured into Yellowstone National Park. The railroad ended then at Glendive, Montana Territory, where Haynes continued by horse and wagon into the Park. He was so overwhelmed by the scenic and photographic possibilities that he returned home with a request to the Secretary of the Interior for a ten-acre site at the edge of the Firehole River across from Beehive Geyser. Haynes' permit was denied each year until 1884 when he was granted the first concessionaire lease in Yellowstone for the construction of a photographic studio.

His photographic empire grew and by 1885 Haynes purchased a Pullman railroad car. He refurbished it, christened it the "Yellowstone", and began touring the Northern Pacific line from St. Paul and Duluth to Puget Sound expounding his views of Yellowstone. Haynes also recognized the potential need for transportation, lodging and guides into Yellowstone for a beckoning public as the 1890s emerged.

The last decade of the nineteenth century saw continued growth in Yellowstone and beyond its political boundaries. The decade was marked by Henry Ford building his first car; the debut of the first moving picture in New York; the beginning of the Klondike Gold Rush at Bonanza Creek; and statehood for Idaho and Wyoming.

In Yellowstone the Army continued to govern and administrate as six-horse coaches brought visitors to the newly constructed hotels in fashionable style. Journeys to Yellowstone at this time were only for the rich, adventuresome and often foreign visitors. One English traveler, Georgina Synge, in her book, *A Ride Through Wonderland*, described her journey into the Upper Geyser Basin in 1891. She wrote, "At the upper end of the geyser basin stands a most civilized-looking hotel (page 20) in Queen Anne style, and quite a sprinkling of people were to be seen about. Some of the female portion thereof were rather elaborately attired for such a remote portion of the globe; and one of them clad in an elegant velvet dolman, high-heeled shoes, and much curled fringe, regarded my buck-skin leggings through her pince-nez, with cold and withering glances."

As the 1890s merged into the new century, Yellowstone continued to see rapid growth in the building of hotels, roads and services. Old Faithful Inn (page 44 and 45) was constructed during the winter of 1903-1904 and opened its doors to the public that following spring. But those doors were still remote from the outside world where Orville and Wilbur Wright were successfully flying a powered airplane; where Richard Steiff was designing the first teddy bears (named after President Theodore Roosevelt); where the Ford Motor Company began producing the first Model T; and where Robert E. Peary was striving to reach the North Pole.

The railroads by then had extended their tracks to the edges of the Park, making it more accessible to Easterners. One Eastern author, F. Dumont Smith, even described in his *Book of a Hundred Bears* the simplistic approach to Yellowstone as, "To arrive to Yellowstone and all its felicities you go to Ogden and turn to the right."

But once visitors arrived here they discovered surprising amenities and service. Upon arriving at Old Faithful, for example, passengers were unloaded, they and their baggage were shuffled to their rooms where they washed in porcelain basins, refreshed, then toured the geyser basin before dinner. Baron of beef, fresh garden vegetables and French wines were served while a quartet played Mozart in the upper 'Crows Nest', allowing the music to filter down to the lobby and through the dining room.

The day's journey from hotel to hotel — or between geyser basins — provided luxury enroute as Dumont Smith wrote of lunch at Norris. "The table was set with beautiful silver, exquisite napery, and shaded candles . . . the dinner . . . it began with a bisque of tomato, smooth as its porcelain namesake; then a great planked whitefish; a saute of chicken livers; a broiled squab with a punch of Marashino that Sherry could not surpass; a green salad; a Nesselrode pudding; black coffee and real Camembert cheese."

By the 1910s the industrial age began to grasp the nation, and we looked beyond our borders to world affairs. During this decade China abolished slavery; the S.S. Titanic sank on her maiden voyage after colliding with an iceberg; zippers became popular (they were first introduced in 1891); and World War I began and ended.

By this decade Yellowstone was not the only national park. Other parks had been established, and by presidential decree, President Theodore Roosevelt (page 32) had formed national monuments for the protection of geologic anomalies and historic sites. It became apparent in 1916 that the U.S. Army could not administer these vast and diverse holdings, and two years later the National Park Service, with their rangers, relieved the soldiers of their duties and took over the administration of Yellowstone.

The year the National Park Service was established is also significant in that it was the year Jack Ellis Haynes assumed responsibility for his father's photography and park concession business.

Jack Haynes, born in Fargo, Dakota Territory, graduated from the University of Minnesota as a mining engineer. He took over his father's business in 1916 and moved to rapidly adapt the family business to changing technologies. But Jack never lived up to his father's expectations. F. Jay Haynes criticized Jack's work and downgraded it in comparison to William Jackson's. Jack did, however, recognize the changing times and influences Yellowstone was undergoing. He saw the advent of the automobile, which ushered people into the Park on their own, without the need of guides, hotels, and public transport. He saw the need for tourist cabins (page 54), auto camps (page 62), guide books, and postcards — all for the self-help, self-contained auto camper.

The 1920s brought prohibition and the smuggling of Canadian whiskey, bound for the dude ranches of Jackson, through the Park along lodgepole-lined roads. The decade also witnessed Lord Carnarvon and Howard Carter's discovery of the tomb of Tutankhamen; Charles A. Lindbergh's nonstop flight from New York to Paris in his monoplane, "Spirit of St. Louis"; the St. Valentine's Day Massacre of six notorious Chicago gangsters machine-gunned to death by a rival gang; and Black Friday when the New York Stock Exchange collapsed, U.S. securities lost $26 billion and the world economic crisis began.

Also during this decade, on the outskirts of Yellowstone a battle raged over the establishment of a national park for the Tetons. The new Yellowstone superintendent, Horace Albright, discovered that because of embittered opposition, conventional means of protecting the Teton landscape would not work. When philanthropist John D. Rockefeller Jr. vacationed in the Yellowstone area, Albright lead him to the Tetons for his first visit. Rockefeller was so impressed by the grandeur of the mountains he believed they should be protected along with the valley floor. After Rockefeller returned home to New York he asked Albright to draw up a map of the private land in the valley and the estimated cost of its purchase. Using profits from the Standard Oil Company, the Snake River Land Company purchased most of the private land on the valley floor. The land was eventually given to the public and, together with the mountain range, Grand Teton National Park was formally incorporated by Congress in 1950.

The next decade, the Great Depression years of the 1930s, took its toll on the world, the nation and upon Yellowstone too. People looked beyond their own misfortunes and sympathized with others whose tragedies were greater than their own during a decade marked by the kidnapping of the Lindbergh baby; the disappearance of Amelia Earhart during her trans-Pacific flight; the disaster of the dirigible Hindenburg at Lakehurst, New Jersey; and persecution of Jews in Europe preceding World War II.

They were tough years in Yellowstone and equally tough for the inhabitants who had settled to farm and ranch in the valleys north and east of the park. The Great Depression years were also associated with Franklin D. Roosevelt (page 90 and 91) and his government aid programs. The Civilian Conservation Corps (CCC) and predator control programs sprang from these New Deal assistance programs. The CCC provided badly needed jobs for men who left their family farms to earn wages through strenuous physical work. But their labors during those years helped build roads, bridges, museums and trails.

Even though the CCC provided valuable assistance to the park the predator control programs did not. During those lean years when livestock and wildlife losses were great it was believed that reducing predators would lessen the losses sustained by ranchers. A war was declared on predators — the coyote, the mountain lion, and the wolf — and a bounty was paid by the government for their hides. When this did not sufficiently reduce their numbers government salaried hunters systematically tracked and hunted them down. The coyote, the most cunning and elusive of the predators, survived; the mountain lion was nearly eliminated; but the wolf lost the war. Wolves were eliminated from the park by the early 1930s. The last one in the region, a pure white northern Rocky Mountain wolf, eluded hunters for years until it too was killed in central Montana in the mid 1930s.

Tourists who ventured to Yellowstone came in two distinct classes – those who could afford first class accomodations and the luxuries the hotels provided and those who provided their own meager transport and tents. They were known as dudes (page 89) and sagebrushers (page 81).

By the 1940s, problems with the economy eased, but the nation plunged into World War II when the Japanese bombed Pearl Harbor. The decade evolved around the events of the war. It was marked by the first atomic bomb detonation near Alamogordo, New Mexico; the saddening news of the war dead estimated at 35 million plus an additional 10 million in Nazi concentration camps; and a U.S. Air Force jet setting a transcontinental record of three hours and forty-six minutes.

As in the nation, events in Yellowstone also evolved around the events of the war. Yellowstone

Park rangers began enlisting in the armed forces and left one by one. Most never returned.

Visitation dropped, and with that the grand old hotels — Old Faithful Inn, Canyon Hotel and Lake Hotel — were boarded up. What few visitors the park saw during the war years, mainly service men traveling cross-country to report to active service and their duty stations, found hospitality, a small cabin, and home cooked meals served in the kitchens of Haynes' Photo Shops and Hamilton Stores only at Mammoth and Old Faithful.

After the war, renewed prosperity came to the national parks. The hotels were given fresh coats of paint and new furnishings for the rooms. New boilers were installed. And college students were once again bound for Yellowstone to spend their summer vacations as waiters, cooks, maids, and bellmen rather than as soldiers fighting on the battle fields of Europe.

As the golden age of black and white photography entered its last decade in 1950, it saw a decade of transition as television sets in the U.S. increased from 1.5 million at the beginning of the decade to over 85 million by its end; it also saw Rock and Roll music and dance sweep the nation; the coronation of Queen Elizabeth II; and the U.S. recognition of Vietnam and the supply of arms and the instructions for their use.

The war years were over and the boom years began. The 1950s were no longer the "fix and repair" years in Yellowstone as they had been directly after the war. Old hotels were torn down or replaced with modern motor lodges. Air transportation brought visitors to the park in a matter of hours, and car camping (page 99) became popular once again. Bobby socks, rolled-up Wranglers, Indian headdresses and rubber tomahawks were the "craze" in Yellowstone.

These photographs conjure images of that golden era of black and white photography. Is it still possible to taste the flying dust of horse drawn coaches, to feel the silkiness of the flappers' pongee dresses, to smell the lodgepole smoke of a camper's fire, and to faintly hear the rumble of an Old Faithful eruption amidst a gathering crowd? Those times are gone and Yellowstone has evolved, but still the images remain.

Carl Schreier
Yellowstone National Park

YELLOWSTONE
SELECTED PHOTOGRAPHS

2   Artist Thomas Moran on Mammoth Terraces, 1871

Pulpit Terrace, 1872   3

4   U.S. Geological Survey with pack train showing the
manner in which all parties traverse these wilds, 1871

Tower Creek, 1871   5

6   Upper Firehole from the crater of Old Faithful, 1878

Old Faithful Geyser, 1878   7

8   Crystal Cascade, above the falls, 1878

Left: Keppler's Cascade, 1878

Right: Cascade Creek (Crystal Falls), 1878

9

10   Craters of the Gourd, Shield and Minute Man, Shoshone Basin, 1878

Crater of the Fountain, Lower Firehole, 1878 11

12   President Chester A. Arthur and Party at Old Faithful, 1883

Wm C. McClintock Group, Lebanon, Ohio. Liberty Cap, Cottage Hotel, Mammoth Hotel in background, 1888   13

14   The Gibbon Falls, 1882

Interior Mammoth Cave, tourists explore
underground in the Devil's Kitchen area, 1884   15

16   Mammoth Hot Springs, 1878

Hot Spring Cone (Fishing Cone), c. 1883   17

18   Lower Falls from Red Rock Winter
      (Grand Canyon of the Yellowstone), January 1887

Our Sketch Artist - Winter (Norris Geyser Basin), January 1887   19

20   Upper Geyser Basin from Beehive Cone.
        Man looking into Beehive, c. 1888

Excelsior Geyser in eruption
(last year of known eruptions), 1888

22   F.J. Haynes in lead of Co. D of Minnesota National Guard
      at Yancey's. He is riding "Rock" and leading "Rye", 1893

Co. C Minnesota National Guard,   23
Musicians, (Rear of Mammoth Hotel), 1893

24   Bicyclist's group on Minerva Terrace.
James A. Moss, Fort Missoula, Montana, October 7, 1896

Soda Butte Soldier Station, 1905   25

26   Camping on Yellowstone Lake, 1882

Hot Spring Cone, Yellowstone Lake (Fishing Cone), c. 1890   27

28   Corkscrew Bridge, Sylvan Pass, n.d.

Canyon Hotel waiters and Yellowstone River, 1896   29

30   Little Firehole Falls (Mystic Falls), 1878

Tourists viewing the Grand Canyon
from platform at brink of falls, 1886   31

32   President Theodore Roosevelt with Capt. Pitcher
      on arrival at the Cinnabar Depot, April 1903

Stages at Gardiner Rail Depot, 1915   33

34   Kitchen of Shaw and Powell Camping Company, c. 1910

Frederick Morris Party and Old Faithful Inn,
Upper Geyser Basin, August 16, 1913

Four-horse coach (M-Y) at glimpse of Upper Falls, 1900

Along the Gibbon River, c. 1903   37

38   Canyon Hotel Lounge from office, 1913

Coaching Party at Canyon Hotel, c. 1915   39

40   Store at Lake Hotel, 1907

Steamer "Zillah" near lake dock,   41
tourists on board, Yellowstone Lake, c. 1904

42   Steamer "Zillah" at dock. E.C. Waters
on dock with his house in the background, c. 1904

Lake Hotel entrance. Manager,
center, John O'Dowd at right, 1904

44   Old Faithful Inn, east front (three men), 1904

Old Faithful Inn barroom, c. 1905   45

46   Bears feeding "A La Carte", n.d.

The Silver Gate, near Mammoth Hot Springs, c. 1908   47

48   Handkerchief Pool, n.d.

Auto at Old Faithful Geyser, 1916   49

50   Fording Pebble Creek, c. 1913

Along the Yellowstone River,
Hayden Valley, July 1916

Interior Fort Yellowstone barracks, 1916

Firing salute gun, July 4, 1916   53

54   Lake Camp cabin (cutaway), 1927

Old Faithful Camp, 1923   55

56   Old Faithful Inn and surroundings, c. 1925

Old Faithful Inn fireplace and lobby, c. 1919   57

58   Tourist Bus at Punch Bowl Spring, 1917

Crater Fountain Geyser, n.d.   59

60   Try and get it, c. 1921

Lewis Falls, c. 1922   61

62   Tourists in Camp, tent campers, 1924

Mrs. Zukar, oldest woman in Cooke City, Montana, 1923   63

64   President Coolidge and party, 1927

Old Faithful Inn with autos and people in front, 1920   65

66   Visitors awaiting Old Faithful Geyser eruption, 1925

Crowd at Giant Geyser cone, 1923   67

68   White-man-runs-him (right) and Max Big Man (left),
      interpreter (Crow Chief), August 10, 1927

Tourists at top of Mt. Washburn, 1924   69

70   Boats at Lake Hotel boat dock, 1922

Appolinaris Spring, E.J. Larkin (left)   71
and Arthur Rule (right), 1925

72   A forced landing at Lake, c. 1925

Ranger-naturalist Herma Albertson
at Mammoth, September 1929

74   Rutted roads in Lamar Valley, c. 1927

Gardiner's Hole, Swan Lake Valley and
Gallatin Range from Kingman Pass, August 25, 1925

76   Lower Falls of the Yellowstone
from Artist's Point, c. 1925

Inspiration Point, President Warren G. Harding   77
and party descending stairway, 1923

78   Early visitors at Handkerchief Pool, c. 1923

Campsite at Mammoth Campground, 1922   79

80   Lake Public Auto Camp party, April 23, 1928

Tourist car at Mammoth Camp, 1924   81

82   Visitors on Uncle Tom's Trail, Canyon, 1922

Lower Falls from Red Rock, 1926　83

84   Yellowstone Park visitors at Dragon's Mouth Spring, 1937

Buses at Norris Geyser Basin Museum, 1937   85

86   Tourists in Old Faithful Swimming Pool, 1936

Old Faithful Swimming Pool, autos and tourists, 1934　　87

88   House of antlers with Mrs. J.E. Haynes
and Mr. and Mrs. Joseph Joffe, c. 1935

Tourists on Terrace Trail, 1936   89

President and Mrs. F.D. Roosevelt tour the Park, 1937

The Roosevelts at Old Faithful, 1937　　91

92   Red Spouter Mudpot, c. 1954

Golden Gate Canyon highway from above, 1948   93

94   Old Faithful Geyser and tourists, 1947

Riverside Geyser, 1949   95

96   Approaching Old Faithful Inn, from the balcony, c. 1951

Canyon Hotel Dining Room, July 6, 1952   97

98   Black bear raiding garbage can, 1961

Family playing cards in Fishing Bridge
Campground, August 22, 1958   99

National Park Service boat "Pelican"
offshore Molly Islands, July 5, 1957

Pod of young pelicans at Molly Islands in
Southwest Arm of Yellowstone Lake, c. 1958

102   Soliciting goodies from bus passengers, September 18, 1960

Fishermen at Fishing Bridge, July 20, 1957   103

104   Visitors at Mammoth Hot Springs, c. 1958

Old Faithful Geyser, 1951

106   Tower Falls, c. 1952

PHOTOGRAPHIC CREDITS

Page   2   W.H. Jackson, Courtesy National Park Service, Yellowstone National Park

3   W.H. Jackson, Colorado Historical Society

4   W.H. Jackson, Colorado Historical Society

5   W.H. Jackson, Colorado Historical Society

6   W.H. Jackson, Colorado Historical Society

7   W.H. Jackson, Colorado Historical Society

8   W.H. Jackson, Colorado Historical Society

9   (left) W.H. Jackson, Colorado Historical Society

9   (right) W.H. Jackson, Colorado Historical Society

10   W.H. Jackson, Colorado Historical Society

11   W.H. Jackson, Colorado Historical Society

12   F.J. Haynes, Courtesy National Park Service, Yellowstone National Park

13   F.J. Haynes, Haynes Foundation Collection, Montana Historical Society

14   F.J. Haynes, Haynes Foundation Collection, Montana Historical Society

15   F.J. Haynes, Haynes Foundation Collection, Montana Historical Society

16   W.H. Jackson, Colorado Historical Society

17   Anonymous, Denver Public Library Western Collection

18   F.J. Haynes, Haynes Foundation Collection, Montana Historical Society

19   F.J. Haynes, Haynes Foundation Collection, Montana Historical Society

20   F.J. Haynes, Haynes Foundation Collection, Montana Historical Society

Page 49 J.E. Haynes, Haynes Foundation Collection, Montana Historical Society

50 Engineer, Department of War, Courtesy National Park Service, Yellowstone National Park

51 J.E. Haynes, Haynes Foundation Collection, Montana Historical Society

52 Anonymous, Courtesy National Park Service, Yellowstone National Park

53 J.E. Haynes, Haynes Foundation Collection, Montana Historical Society

54 J.E. Haynes, Haynes Foundation Collection, Montana Historical Society

55 Anonymous, Courtesy Homer Noar, Union Pacific Railroad

56 Anonymous, Courtesy National Archives

57 J.E. Haynes, Haynes Foundation Collection, Montana Historical Society

58 J.E. Haynes, Haynes Foundation Collection, Montana Historical Society

59 W.H. Jackson, Colorado Historical Society

60 Anonymous, Courtesy American Heritage Center, University of Wyoming

61 Anonymous, Courtesy American Heritage Center, University of Wyoming

62 Anonymous, Courtesy National Park Service, Yellowstone National Park

63 Franz, Courtesy National Park Service, Yellowstone National Park

64 Anonymous, Courtesy National Park Service, Yellowstone National Park

65 J.E. Haynes, Courtesy National Park Service, Yellowstone National Park

66 Anonymous, Courtesy National Park Service, Yellowstone National Park

67 J.E. Haynes, Haynes Foundation Collection, Montana Historical Society

68 J.E. Haynes, Haynes Foundation Collection, Montana Historical Society

69 Anonymous, Courtesy National Park Service, Yellowstone National Park

70 Anonymous, Courtesy National Park Service, Yellowstone National Park

71 J.E. Haynes, Haynes Foundation Collection, Montana Historical Society

72 Anonymous, Courtesy Homer Noar, Union Pacific Railroad

73 Joseph Joffe, Courtesy National Park Service, Yellowstone National Park

74 Anonymous, Courtesy National Park Service, Yellowstone National Park

75 J.E. Haynes, Haynes Foundation Collection, Montana Historical Society

76 Anonymous, Courtesy Homer Noar, Union Pacific Railroad

77 Anonymous, Courtesy National Park Service, Yellowstone National Park

78 Anonymous, Courtesy National Park Service, Yellowstone National Park

79 Anonymous, Courtesy National Park Service, Yellowstone National Park

80 J.E. Haynes, Haynes Foundation Collection, Montana Historical Society

Page 81   Cribbs, Courtesy National Park Service, Yellowstone National Park

82   Anonymous, Courtesy National Park Service, Yellowstone National Park

83   J.E. Haynes, Haynes Foundation Collection, Montana Historical Society

84   J.E. Haynes, Haynes Foundation Collection, Montana Historical Society

85   J.E. Haynes, Haynes Foundation Collection, Montana Historical Society

86   J.E. Haynes, Haynes Foundation Collection, Montana Historical Society

87   J.E. Haynes, Haynes Foundation Collection, Montana Historical Society

88   J.E. Haynes, Haynes Foundation Collection, Montana Historical Society

89   J.E. Haynes, Haynes Foundation Collection, Montana Historical Society

90   International News Photo, Courtesy National Archives

91   Anonymous, Courtesy Wyoming State Archives, Museums and Historical Department

92   Anonymous, Courtesy Homer Noar, Union Pacific Railroad

93   J.E. Haynes, Haynes Foundation Collection, Montana Historical Society

94   B.L. Brown, Haynes Foundation Collection, Montana Historical Society

95   J.E. Haynes, Haynes Foundation Collection, Montana Historical Society

96   Anonymous, Courtesy Homer Noar, Union Pacific Railroad

97   J.E. Haynes, Haynes Foundation Collection, Montana Historical Society

98   Anonymous, Courtesy National Park Service, Yellowstone National Park

99   Teisberg, Courtesy National Park Service, Yellowstone National Park

100   Beal, Courtesy National Park Service, Yellowstone National Park

101   David de L. Condon, Courtesy National Park Service, Yellowstone National Park

102   McIntyre, Courtesy National Park Service, Yellowstone National Park

103   Teisberg, Courtesy National Park Service, Yellowstone National Park

104   Anonymous, Courtesy National Park Service, Yellowstone National Park

105   J.E. Haynes, Haynes Foundation Collection, Montana Historical Society

106   George L. Beam, Denver Public Library Western History Department